Washington, D.C.

United States Capitol at Night

Table of Contents

Introduction 6

Emergence of a City 7

The Nation Honors Its Heroes 40

Washington, D.C. Today 43

The Words and Photographs
are Copyright © 1986 by
LMPC with Creative Forum Publishing

All Rights Reserved.

Sixth Printing, June 1998

Sands Print Group, Ltd. • Printed in Singapore

Washington, D.C.

by A.L. Carlisle

Photography by James Blank

The White House

United States Capitol

Introduction

Is it possible to take a fresh look at the lives and times of this city on the Potomac River, a city of layers and layers of history as in the tradition of other great cities in the world, such as London and Rome? Think of the voices that have whispered, conversed, cried and shouted within the parameters of Washington, D.C.—inside the stately buildings, through all the time of the city's existence, from the days when Washington was a place composed of wild groves of trees, soft riverbanks, animals, birds and fish to Washington today, populated by people from all over the world, filled with monuments that are legendary, and memorials that are poignant reminders of days that are now dreams and memories.

Power, government and politics are the wheels that have moved this city forward, from the eighteenth century to the present day. Washington, D.C. is the political center of a great world democracy. It is home of the executive mansion, better known to us as the White House, where U.S. presidents and their families have lived for nearly two hundred years. This nation's laws are made in Congress and its military strategies are planned in the Pentagon.

In this neatly planned city, with its streets that radiate away from the Capitol like spokes away from the hub of a wheel, are the classically perfect Jefferson Memorial and the imposing Washington Monument. It is apropos of their position as founders of the city and the nation that Jefferson and Washington are so honored. The Lincoln Memorial is another tribute to greatness. To visit these places is to come to know more deeply these men who have contributed so much to the material and spiritual growth of this country.

Gathering together many of the mementos of events and legendary figures in America is the collection at the Smithsonian Institution—an institution like the others in Washington that *is* America—and which certainly delineates more than anything all the twists and turns of this country. Nearly as impossible as perceiving everything that is or has ever happened in the city itself would be to see and assimilate everything in the Smithsonian Institution.

Our goal here is to give you a new look at this city and to make things just a little more complete for you in your own pictures and ideas about Washington, D.C., so that the next time you read about it or hear it mentioned on the 6 o'clock news, or sit dreaming about paying a visit to this historical city, you will conjure up easily something of what you have found in this book.

Emergence of a City from the Woods

"Here Sir, the people govern." ALEXANDER HAMILTON

The obvious place to begin to know any city is at its origins. Looking upon Washington D.C. from such heights as, for example, the Washington Monument, one marvels at the beauty of it. Surely, it seems, this city of classical architecture has been here forever, but it is even more marvelous to note that where this elegant capital now exists there was no city at all only two hundred years ago. The capital was not appointed in an already existing city; it was planned and created from thick woods and a mighty river.

At the end of the Revolutionary War there were five cities in which the new government functioned: New York, Philadelphia, Trenton, Princeton and Annapolis. There was great controversy as to which city should be the national capital.

In 1785, before the Constitution was adopted, a commission appointed by Congress was instructed to find a site on the Delaware for the new nation's capital and to make arrangements for the construction of a house for this new nation's president. No one on the commission acted. The debate raged on until finally it was resolved at a dinner party where two strong factions, one for New York and one for Philadelphia, gave in to the proposal for a new city, a "Federal City," as Washington himself called it. It would be located on the Potomac River. The name Potomac, aptly enough, means "the river of the meeting of the tribes." On July 16, 1790, President Washington signed a bill that officially put the plan for the city into motion.

Washington hired a French-born engineer by the name of Pierre L'Enfant to plan the new city. L'Enfant joined Washington and the surveyors on their expeditions and began to envision what he called "a mighty empire."

L'Enfant was a tall man, and thin, and slightly eccentric. He wore a beaver hat and blue military coat and carried a silver tipped cane. Soon he was alone on his own walks and rides through the forest around the Potomac. He carried with him the maps of European cities that he had been studying and mused to himself about Versailles with its palace, grand avenues, broad vistas and celebrated gardens.

The Frenchman was temperamental and a difficult man to work with. The commission had a hard time with some aspects of his plan but finally agreed that the streets would radiate outward from the Capitol and would be named numerically and in accordance with the alphabet. The alphabetical streets, he decreed, would be those running north and south and the numbered streets would go east and west. This was all well and good, but the vision of an empire was contrary to what they felt to be the nation's purpose. After all, this was a country where the people ruled. It was not meant to be an empire.

L'Enfant, however, felt omnipotent in his position as planner. He wanted his vision and would have it, he thought, no matter what. He stopped submitting his plans for examination and did reckless things such as having a house that was under construction destroyed because it was in the way of the plan.

Rayburn House Office Building

Even George Washington got fed up at last. After mounting frustration the commission wrote L'Enfant with an offer to pay him off and with the declaration that they were cutting their ties with him as their planner.

Shocked, he appealed to Congress for compensation and was paid off with about a thousand dollars. He was unable to make peace with the men he worked with and died in poverty, with the plan for the capital on his person.

Even though the city of Washington is classical in its conception, perhaps the dismissal of L'Enfant was ultimately a symbolic act, the refusal to have the young nation's capital bear the burden of "empire." To give L'Enfant and the early planners their due, it was a great task to build a city in the middle of woods and plantations on unsurveyed territory. The miracle is that despite strife between commissioners and planners (even those following L'Enfant), despite woods, despite arguments between farmers who wanted to plant corn where city streets ought to go and despite the flaring tempers and egos of surveyors and architects, Washington D.C. came forth in marble and granite splendor amidst the green and blue of forest and Potomac.

Designs for the Capitol Building were submitted to a competition that promised $500 as prize. A doctor, William Thornton, decided to put forward his idea for the structure even though he was not trained at all as an architect. Born in the West Indies, Thornton had traveled to England and France for his education. He loved horses, wit and refinement and was more than capable as an artist, poet and inventor. George Washington and his assistants were taken by the simple lines of Thornton's drawings. They named him winner and began to put his plans into motion.

1793 was the 18th year of American independence and September 18, 1793 was a beautiful, clear and bright day. George Washington and his close little band of patriots paraded to the site of the new Capitol accompanied by the slow beat of drums. Their mission was to acknowledge, with Masonic rites, the placement of the corner-stone of the building and, symbolically, of the nation.

Washington laid the cornerstone and upon it put a ceremonial plate covered with corn, oil and wine. Then the whole party went off to have a feast and listen to the celebratory firing of guns and cannons around the city. By 1796, the foundation of the great Capitol Building was in place.

Congress held its first meeting in the Capitol on November 17, 1800. The senate met on November 22 of the same year. Both were convened in the old north wing which was, at the time, the only completed section.

The Capitol stood until August, 1814 when the British took over the city and burned it. The British soldiers used barrels, furniture, books and portraits of Marie Antoinette and Louis XVI to set the blaze.

The fire was ferocious enough to burn many other buildings and trees. Invaluable records were lost including those that were part of the Congressional Library and the secret journal of Congress, along with many, many private letters and documents of historical importance.

Legend has it that William Thornton saved the Patent Office when he saw a British officer about to order the building destroyed. He galloped up to him on his horse, dismounted and shouted, "Are you Englishmen or Goths and Vandals? This is the Patent Office, the depository of the inventive genius of America in which the whole civilized world is concerned. Would

Treasury Building

Supreme Court

11

you destroy it? If so, fire away, and let the charge pass through my body."

The burning of the Capitol and other government buildings stirred up great bitterness in the people of the new nation and friends abroad. In the days that followed the terrible fires, Americans had to assert themselves and begin their rebuilding. It was a young nation and resilient. The Capitol Building was completely rebuilt by 1830 after an architect from Boston, Charles Bulfinch, had devoted a good portion of his life to its restoration.

The dome, made of brick and wood, caught fire in 1851 when the library again burned. It was then replaced by an iron dome painted white but that structure was not completed until 1865. The incredible dome measures 307 feet. It has been compared to the magnificence of St. Peter's in Rome and St. Paul's in London. During its construction walls had to be clamped in place and held by all possible means to assure the security of the 4 ton structure.

Thirty six columns encircle the lower part of the dome's exterior, representing the 36 states that made up the Union at the time it was built. Thirteen columns surrounding the lantern above the tholus symbolize the 13 colonies. The lantern was placed here to signal to the citizens of Washington that there was a night session occurring in the building.

The crowning touch of glory for the majestic dome was the statue called "Freedom." The bronze sculpture was created by Thomas Crawford for a commission of $3000. He made the cast for the statue in his studio in Rome. It arrived in the U.S. on the schooner *Statesman* and was sent to the Clark Mills foundry in Bladensburg and then on to the dome.

It took two weeks to place the 19-1/2 foot statue and when it was at last in place at noon on December 2, 1863, flags were raised and guns were fired all over the city.

Three hundred and sixty five steps twist narrowly upward to the dome and at the top the view includes the cluster of city buildings, broad avenues running one way to the Treasury and the other to the Potomac, red brick steeples and columns of marble, the bright river spotted with sails, Georgetown, and Howard University. On the night President Lincoln was shot, almost under the shadow of the dome and near where Lincoln took his oath of office, John Wilkes Booth rode frantically up New Jersey Avenue toward the bridge and on to Maryland.

Although Freedom was the crown of the Capitol, additions were still made, including a fairly recent (1955) addition of an extension for which President Eisenhower laid the cornerstone.

Approaching the Capitol one first appreciates the exquisite landscaping. Thanks to the genius of Frederick Law Olmsted, the man who created Central Park, the grounds are abundantly flowered and there is a variety of trees including elm, oak, cherry, magnolia and sequoia, as well as shrubbery from Japan and China. Some of the trees are rare and are marked with their names.

The enormous bronze doors at the east front entrance of the Capitol are the work of Randolph Rogers, who used them to depict events in the life of Christopher Columbus. When entering the Capitol it is moving to note that several American leaders and the unknown soldiers have been honored in the rotunda. Visitors came to pay their last respects to Presidents Lincoln and John Kennedy in this room. Above swirl the figures in the fresco painted by an Italian immigrant, Constantine Brumidi, in his "Apotheosis of Washington." Represented in the 4,664 square foot fresco are the thirteen states of the Union, Liberty, Victory and Freedom. A scaffold was raised so the painter could work. He painted using a water-base paint and completed it in just under a year. Brumidi was also the creator of the wall fresco in the Capitol that depicts the country's history.

Some of the paintings that can be seen in the Capitol are *The Embarkation of the Pilgrims* by Robert W. Weir, *Surrender of Cornwallis* by Trumbull, *The Declaration of Independence* by Trumbull, *George Washington* by Rembrandt Peale, *Washington at Yorktown* by Brumidi, *Lincoln and the Emancipation Proclamation* by Francis B. Carpenter and the mural, *Westward the Course of Empire Takes its Way* by Emanuel Leutz. Appropriately, the walls of the Capitol contain the pictorial record of the nation's early history.

In addition to the paintings, there is other elegance to recommend a tour of the Capitol for visual pleasure alone, not to mention the workings of the government which occur here. There are many marble fireplaces, chandeliers, bronze busts and figures, the Brumidi Corridor painted with birds and flowers and colorful tiles, arched ceilings, antiques, gilded mirrors and velvet draperies.

Speeches brilliant with declarations on behalf of freedom and the ideals of the country have been spoken within these walls. This is a building that is the site of hard work in maintaining and pushing forward the nation's business. The rooms of the Senate and the House with their curved seating and balconies have been the scene of debate, celebration, sorrow and challenge.

Reminding the visitor of both the history that has taken place here and the wit and wisdom of eminent Americans are the many statues in the corridors of the great building. Everyone from President Grant to Will Rogers can be met in the form of a statue. Moving along these same corridors are the living workers of today's American political story, men and women from the Senate and Congress. They walk to their daily work alongside tourists, lobbyists, visitors and pages. Senate and House office buildings are located close by. The Senate's buildings are to the northeast and the House buildings are to the south. In order of their completion these buildings are: The Cannon House, the Old Senate Office Building, Longworth House, the New Senate Office Building and the Rayburn House Office Building. This last building was named for the Texan, Sam Rayburn, Speaker of the House for three terms.

The Capitol is the place of inaugurations. James Monroe was the first President to take the oath out of doors. Andrew Jackson's inauguration took place before an enormous audience, most of whom were terribly enthusiastic. For a time the city was taken over by over 10,000 visitors who could not withhold their joy at seeing "Old Hickory" in office. They ran wild through the halls of the Capitol and over the lawns of the White House.

Perhaps the most awesome and cherished building in the nation's history is the Capitol. It was the dream of the new nation's first architects of freedom to have a building grand enough to reflect their vision. Today, Americans continue to look to the workers in this building to insure the safekeeping of that original vision.

Near the Capitol is one of the more splendid places to visit in the world, the National Botanic Gardens. This is a good place to go on a rainy day or when tired of walking through buildings. A visitor to the city might like to be lost among full grown grapefruit trees and tropical plants for a change, or tread carefully through a room full of cacti. In this conservatory are orchid displays, ferns, rubber plants, and changing seasonal and holiday displays.

Lafayette Square

The White House

In the spring there is a beautiful display of flowering bulbs such as daffodils, tulips, iris and every possible kind of early spring flower that blooms.

In front of the Capitol, between Independence and Constitution Avenues is a park-like strip known as the Mall. This long stretch of greenery is looked upon by important public buildings and monuments. Probably the most exciting day to be here is on the Fourth of July. At the Capitol end of the Mall the National Symphony Orchestra plays patriotic music during a display of fireworks that bursts over the Washington Monument. Those interested in a closer look at the dazzle of it all will want to stand as close to the great obelisk as possible and see the spectacular colors blaze and fade against the dark sky.

On less eventful days there is plenty of stimulation around the Mall. For one thing, there is the Smithsonian. An Englishman, James Smithson, son of the Duke of Northumberland, left a bequest to the United States of half a million dollars. He stated that he wanted it to be used to create an "establishment for the increase and diffusion of knowledge among men." His gift was used to build the Smithsonian Institution. Its first building, now called the Castle because of its towers and turrets, is a beautiful old building designed by James Renwick. It is now the center for a number of other buildings which are dedicated to the same purpose including the following: The Museum of Natural History, the Freer Gallery, the Arts and Industries building, the Hirshhorn Museum, the National Zoological Park, the Renwick Gallery, the Museum of African Art, the John F. Kennedy Center, the Astrophysical Observatory, the Archives of American Art, and the National Gallery of Art.

Children stand in hushed wonder before the dinosaurs on display in the Museum of Natural History. This building contains records of life from the prehistoric to the present, including insect life. Also on view is the blue-white Hope diamond, among thousands of other gems in the gem collection. Stuffed birds and animals in woodland scenes are abundant but perhaps the most striking animal on display is the stuffed elephant on an oval patch of simulated African desert standing in the rotunda, surrounded, unlikely enough, by marble pillars. There are exhibits of America's Indians, various tribes shown living as they did before the country was settled by pioneers. All in all, there are over 60,000,000 items collected in this museum.

Not to be missed as part of the Smithsonian empire is the National Air and Space Museum. Missiles, rockets and airplanes are the theme. Approaching, you can see some of the aircraft through gigantic windows. Inside, the aircraft on view includes everything from the Wright Brothers' aircraft to jet planes to nosecones and helium balloons. Even if the visitor is not interested in technology, the museum is fascinating. You can learn how a jet engine really works and stand in a mini-theatre watching a short film that shows, from the pilot's point of view, a jet approaching National airport, flying low and fast over the Potomac and the Kennedy Center.

The Freer Gallery and the Hirshhorn Museum are also part of the Smithsonian. The Hirshhorn was started with a collection donated by the millionaire Joseph Hirshhorn. He collected modern art and this is the focus, in painting and sculpture, for this museum. The Freer Gallery was established to contain the impressive collection of Oriental art owned by Charles

Washington Monument

Monument and Reflecting Pool

Lincoln Memorial

Lincoln Memorial at Dusk

View from Lincoln Memorial

Lincoln Memorial

Museum of American History

22

Smithsonian Institute

(Overleaf) Jefferson Memorial

26 Shrine of Immaculate Conception

Washington Cathedral

The Watergate Complex

Botanical Gardens

Lincoln Memorial

Jefferson Memorial at Night

Freer. The gallery looks like a royal home, designed in a Florentine-Renaissance style by Charles A. Platt.

Across the Mall from the National Air and Space Museum is the National Gallery of Art. Andrew Mellon, formerly Secretary of the Treasury in the early half of the century, donated art from his own extensive collection to help create the National Gallery. The collection was quickly added to, thanks to other donations, and finally another gallery had to be built to contain it all. This structure is called the East Building of the National Gallery. It was designed by I.M. Pei. It is a large, open, soaring space with a giant Calder mobile hanging from the ceiling. The elevator goes to the top of the tower where there is a selection of Matisse paper cutouts.

One way to go from the new wing to the old wing is through an underground passageway on a moving sidewalk. As you come out of the subterranean world you emerge into a refreshing scene. A cascade of water falls to your right. The water comes down from above over a giant sheet of glass.

Mark Twain called the Smithsonian "the nation's attic." It has come to be much more than that. The Smithsonian includes the living, not only fascinating relics from the past. For example, the Kennedy Center for the Performing Arts brings the most exciting performers in the world to work in this city. The National Zoological Park, once a few cages for animals given by other countries to the President, is now one of the largest zoos on the east coast. The two wonderful darlings of the zoo are the pandas, gifts from China. If you get there at feeding time, you can see the big bears eating their snacks of bamboo, pulling off one strip at a time with their thumb and finger, looking just like giant teddy bears. When the pandas are mating, newscasters in Washington, D.C. discuss it every night on the 6 o'clock news.

North of the Mall is the area known as the Federal Triangle. It includes many of the departments and agencies that run the federal government. Most of the buildings in this complex were erected between 1930 and 1937. These buildings include the Federal Trade Commission, the National Archives, the Department of Justice, the Internal Revenue Service, Coast Guard Headquarters, the District of Columbia Municipal Building and Bell, the Department of Commerce and the Department of Labor.

Of this group of buildings, one of the most popular for visitors is the National Archives. Stored here are the documents that gave language to the early American ideals of independence and freedom. Displayed under glass and protected by helium are the Declaration of Independence, the Bill of Rights and the Constitution. This enormous building is where historians and scholars have studied this country's origins for the past half century. John Russell Pope, the man who designed the building, also designed the Jefferson Memorial. The National Archives also contain family genealogies, Indian treaties and parchment declarations made by presidents as far back as Washington.

At the end of the eighteenth century it was obvious that the country needed some sort of library to contain records and resources for the work of Congress. As a response to this need, the Library of Congress was established and, even though much of its contents were twice destroyed by fire, it rose from the ashes. After the first fire, Jefferson replaced many of the volumes lost with books from his personal library. He asked $23,000 for his contribution and the government gave it to

Viet Nam Memorial

Marine Corps War Memorial

him. Unfortunately, much of that library was destroyed in the second fire, but this time, in 1851, Congress started it again with $100,000. The Library has been growing ever since.

Once part of the Capitol Building, the Library of Congress now has its own structure, an elaborately detailed French Renaissance building, an annex and another building, the latter two added in this century.

Used extensively to respond to Congressional queries, the Library has a reputation as a home for research with a wide range of subjects. Over 80,000,000 pieces of information reside here in the form of books, pamphlets, microfilm, folios of sheet music recordings, and maps. It is the location of the U.S. Copyright Office.

The great marble temple of justice, the Supreme Court, is the place of final appeal by the people of this country. It is meant to be the ultimate in human justice. Once the Court was required to meet within the walls of the Capitol Building, but was given its own structure, designed by Cass Gilbert, in 1935. It was intended to resemble the edifices of ancient Greece. Two seated figures are on either side of the flight of white steps leading to the entrance. Above them is the single statement, "Equal Justice Under Law." One of the figures considers justice while the other considers its execution under the law. The bronze doors designed by John Donnelly weigh 6 tons. Guided tours are available and the court meets on the first Monday of October through the spring. Visitors may attend weekday sessions if room permits.

Nearby is one of Washington's most interesting libraries, the Folger Shakespeare Library. It is devoted to English history and the literature written between the years 1476 and 1715. Its purpose has been to study this era. Many of the ideas and philosophies born in the Elizabethan times deeply affected the minds of the people responsible for what was to become the United States. The building has an Elizabethan interior. Several early editions of Shakespeare's work are kept here and other items that allow us to know this important age, including 250,000 volumes of prose and poetry.

Leaving the Mall, one is naturally drawn to the nearby White House. Once both patriotic citizens and the curious could enter the White House by walking through the front door. They ventured through hallways in search of the President, either to just see him or have a word with him. There was no Secret Service and, as far as the building was concerned, no security guards. Today the building is still open to the public, but the whole White House is not available for wandering through and, as we all know, the President is kept carefully guarded.

Designed by James Hoban, the building sits on a meticulously landscaped acreage with gardens, fountains and well-groomed shrubbery. The famous Rose Garden has been the scene of countless press conferences and talks with visiting dignitaries. This house has been the home of every U.S. President since John Adams and virtually every President has added to or subtracted from the decor according to personal taste and/or a personal sense of historic priorities.

The President's family is housed on the second floor, while the West Wing is the scene of daily political and national business and is where the President meets official visitors. The East Wing is where the first lady traditionally meets guests. State rooms are called by colors—the Green, Blue and Red Rooms—plus the State Dining Room.

The Diplomatic Reception Room, entered from the ground floor on the south side of the White House was the scene of Franklin Roosevelt's "fireside chats," when he talked with Americans over the radio. Refurbished by Jackie Kennedy, this is now a gracefully appointed room with an 1834 mural by Jean Zuber et Cie in Alsace entitled "Scenic America."

Even though it is not as easy as it once was to visit the President, thousands come to the White House every year. The grounds are protected by an iron fence and the Secret Service is everywhere, but still they come because, guarded or not, this house and this personage belong to the people.

Across the street from the White House is Lafayette Square, named after the French general who supported America's independence in the Revolutionary War. L'Enfant had thought the White House should have an enormous park around it but Jefferson thought the house grand enough and had Pennsylvania Avenue extended instead. For a long time the area that is now Lafayette Square was a racetrack, then a zoo. Finally, in 1816, it became the site of St. John's Church.

The church brought the gentry forward. They could see the brilliance of surrounding the White House with their own homes and so the Square became the celebrated neighborhood of the elite. Everyone who has been a participant in Washington politics has either lived on the Square or visited.

Some of the residents were more notorious then others. Commodore Stephen Decatur, for example, was a dramatic man who died in a duel. Daniel Sickles, a statesman, moved into the Square in the middle of the nineteenth century. He had a beautiful Italian wife and imagined that she was faithful to him. She, however, fell in love with the son of Frances Scott Key, Philip, and they carried on a clandestine affair until Sickles found out and killed the young Key as he walked home across the Square. Sickles was not found guilty of murder. He went on to gather up other honors, including a post as Minister of Spain. His marriage endured.

In Lafayette Park stands a statue of Andrew Jackson on horseback. This bronze statue, sculpted by Clark Mills, is made from the cannon Jackson took from the British during the Battle of Pensacola in the War of 1812. Other statues of Revolutionary leaders are also here: Lafayette, Rochambeau, Kosciusko and von Steuben.

Washington, D.C. has valued and carefully preserved its past: When the British were burning the Capitol, Mrs. Monroe fled the White House with Gilbert Stuart's portrait of George Washington and as many other historical treasures as she could manage. The house where President Lincoln died, called the Peterson House, still stands and is still visited by those interested in history. Ford's Theatre where Lincoln was shot is still in existence. Guided tours of the buildings we have mentioned are available to visitors who wish to better understand the country's history. And everywhere, all around the city, are the monuments and memorials that acknowledge the country's leaders and those who have contributed to America's rich and fascinating history.

Tomb of Unknown Soldier

The Nation Honors Its Heroes

There are monuments great and small in Washington, D.C. Some stand tall and clear against the skyline, such as the Washington Monument, and others are small and rarely noticed, such as the marker in Franklin Roosevelt's honor near the National Archives Building. Those most visited, best loved and treasured by visitors to the capital and citizens of Washington, D.C. itself are the Washington Monument, the Lincoln Memorial, the Jefferson Memorial, Arlington National Cemetery and the Vietnam Memorial.

The Washington Monument, like many government structures from the Capitol Building to the Vietnam Memorial, had its design chosen in a competition. Robert Mills was the winning designer and his monument dedicated to the nation's first president is a pale obelisk that towers against the skyline. Although begun in 1833, the monument was not completed until well after the Civil War because of shortages in funds and problems related to the design.

Opposite, at the other end of the narrow strip of water called the Reflecting Pool, stands the imposing memorial to President Lincoln. The enormous seated statue of the president effectively creates a sense of his greatness. One climbs the long flight of steps with a sense of wonder. Within the memorial are excerpts from Lincoln's inaugural address and the Gettysburg Address engraved in the pale stone. It is very easy, in the presence of his language, to stand still in the shadows and dream the dreams that he gave voice to. For history's sake, it should be noted that Daniel Chester French was the sculptor responsible for the statue and Henry Bacon designed this impressive memorial. At the time of construction there were 48 states in the Union so 48 steps lead to the memorial. The 36 doric columns symbolize the 36 free states of Lincoln's time.

The Jefferson Memorial is south of the Mall. Its dome and circular, pillared exterior are patterned after the architecture Jefferson felt kinship with, especially the Pantheon. The structure rests at the edge of the Tidal Basin and is surrounded by green banners of lawn and trees.

Within the Jefferson Memorial are excerpts from the Declaration of Independence, penned by this brilliant leader and engraved in the stone. John Russell Pope designed the monument but Rudolph Evans created the statue of Jefferson, tall and imposing in a long coat. It is cast in bronze. One feels, reading the words of this man, that he had a great spirit. He was truly a man of his time. A rich landowner and slaveowner, he perhaps wrote the Declaration of Independence in spite of his own best interests.

Hundreds of cherry trees bloom around the Tidal Basin near this memorial. They are celebrated in April by the Cherry Blossom Festival. At this time the Japanese Lantern is lit to begin the festivities. This lantern is made of stone and was sculpted in Japan in 1651. It was given to the United States in 1954 by Japan. Many of the cherry trees were gifts from the Japanese government. Unfortunately, to build the Jefferson Memorial, some of the cherry trees had to be cut down. This broke the hearts of many cherry tree enthusiasts. They saw no reason to destroy the beautiful trees for a man-made monument and so, in the 1930's, debate over this memorial was intense. Some people chained themselves to the trees so

JFK Grave and Arlington House

they would not be cut down, but the builders of the Jefferson Memorial had their way.

To remember those who died performing their service on behalf of this country's defense, the 512 acres of the Arlington National Cemetery are covered with simple white marble markers. On the south bank of the Potomac, the cemetery can be approached via the Memorial Bridge and through the Avenue of Heroes where a statue of Admiral Richard E. Byrd stands.

The history of this cemetery is interesting. It exists because Mrs. Robert E. Lee could not cross the battle lines of the Civil War to pay $96.06 in back taxes on the Lee's huge plantation. The government felt justified in taking some of the land in exchange for the taxes and made it into the cemetery. Since the latter half of the nineteenth century, this has been the final resting place of military men and women, some presidents and other American heroes.

Arlington is the location of the Tomb of the Unknown Soldier, a poignant memorial. Every hour, in a meticulously conducted ceremony, there is a Changing of the Honor Guard. The tomb itself is white marble.

John F. Kennedy is buried in Arlington Cemetery. His grave is marked with the Eternal Flame, a fire that burns in a bronze font that rests on a simple marble base. President Kennedy spoke at Arlington in honor of America's veterans only eleven days before his own death.

Here too is the site of the grave of Pierre L'Enfant, the city's original planner who died in poverty in Maryland. After more than a century, the city wanted to honor him and moved his remains to a gravesite in Arlington.

All Confederate soldiers are buried near each other in Jackson Circle at the Confederate Memorial. In 1914 this memorial was dedicated to them by President Wilson. Prior to this time, their graves were in various sites around the cemetery.

Other famous Americans buried at Arlington Cemetery are General Pershing, General George C. Marshall, Robert Todd Lincoln and Walter Reed. Adjacent to the Arlington National Cemetery is the Marine Corps War Memorial, also known as the Iwo Jima Memorial. Perhaps this creates more powerfully than any other monument a sense of soldiers in action. It was designed by Horace Peaslee after a photograph taken by Joseph Rosenthal of a scene on Iwo Jima. The four Marines and a sailor were raising the U.S. flag on Mount Suribachi after a battle when Rosenthal took their picture. At the base of the statue are the dates of significant Marine battles engaged in since 1775.

The Vietnam Veterans Memorial was designed by a seventeen year old woman and the design was, again, the result of a competition. The long black marble stones, with names of the dead engraved in lists, depict simply and effectively the long dark era of the Vietnam War. Tourists come to see the memorial, but families and friends of the people remembered here come too. They find the names of their own recorded in the book that stands at one end of the monument, then pass slowly along the gleaming marble, their faces reflected in the shining black stone, reading the rows of names. At last they see the name of their friend, their son, brother or husband and instinctively a hand reaches out to touch the stone. Some leave flowers on the ground below; others look for a long time at the name or names they have sought, then slowly move on.

There are many other statues and monuments in Washington that are noteworthy. On the lower terrace of the

Capitol is a statue of John Marshall. Marshall served as Chief Justice of the Supreme Court and was the person who made the court's function be the interpreter of the U.S. constitution.

Another monument to Abraham Lincoln in the form of a statue was sculpted by a young woman, Vinnie Ream. It is also in the Capitol. The story about this statue is that Lincoln allowed this woman to sketch him because he knew she was poor. For five months before his death she sketched him in preparation for her sculpture. Another famous statue by this artist, in honor of Admiral David ("Damn the torpedoes!") Farragut, stands in Lincoln Square.

A large semicircular hall in the Capitol building is known as Statuary Hall. Starting in 1857 the government allowed each state to donate two statues of heroes or patriots. Also, beneath the rotunda of this building are three statues of three women who fought the battle for women's suffrage—Elizabeth Cady Stanton, Susan B. Anthony and Lucretia Mott.

At the foot of Capitol Hill, on the west end stands a memorial to the slain President James Garfield. Garfield had only been in office for six months when a bitter political rival, Charles Guiteau, shot him in a railroad station. The statue depicts the president and three aspects of his life: student, statesman and warrior.

Other important memorials are the U.S. Grant Memorial designed by Henry Shrady, the Peace Memorial erected to honor Navy personnel lost at sea in the Civil War, the 100 foot high marble memorial to President Taft, and the Benjamin Franklin statue, sculpted by Jacques Jouvenal, depicting the old statesman in his formal long coat holding the Treaty of Alliance between the United States and France.

Countless monuments fill this city. One cannot walk very far without seeing statues and plaques, military leaders on horseback, statesmen addressing the crowds, men and women who wrote poetry, saved lives, built buildings, and created a new political structure in the world. Carl Sandburg wrote: "Whenever a people or an institution forgets its early hard beginnings, it is beginning to decay." Washington, D.C. remembers those who made the city and the nation possible.

Washington, D.C. Today

Washington, D.C. is a great sprawling city, a mixture of architecture, a large city with—because of the malls and classical government buildings—a park-like feeling. It is an easy city to get to know and love. It has its outstanding points of national interest as well as a modern urban life that is filled with entertainment and color.

Nearly everyone who comes to Washington has to get a glimpse of the Pentagon. This network of complex corridors is a five sided, five storied structure in which decisions about U.S. defense are made. The building surrounds an inner courtyard and is itself surrounded by parking lots and highways. There are 25,000 people working here. They have their own fire department, post office, department stores, dentists and doctors. Supposedly it takes only 6-1/2 minutes to get from any one point in the Pentagon to another, but that, of course, is true only for those who can find their way around the 17 miles of hallways.

Those most wanted by the Federal Bureau of Investigation are eluding the most elaborate modern technology that

Netherlands Carillon Tower

Georgetown University

exists in the world for tracing criminals. The J. Edgar Hoover Building, now part of the Federal Triangle complex, was built in the 1970's. A tour is a must for anyone interested in exhibits ranging from America's gangster era to criminology laboratories. The tour concludes with a sharpshooting display by agents.

The printing of all the paper money in the United States happens at the Bureau of Engraving and Printing on 14th and C Streets. Because of the elaborate process used to make U.S. money, counterfeiters have repeatedly failed to get it right. $35 million is created daily to replace money that is worn out. Apparently the average dollar bill only lives happily for 18 months before it has to be replaced. This building is also the site where postage stamps, government bonds, licenses and revenue stamps are made.

The Old Post Office in the Federal Triangle was built in 1899. It is a building of distinctive character with a Victorian design. Today it is also called the Pavilion and has been converted into restaurants and shops. There are lots of concession stands here as well as fine restaurants. A large central seating area accommodates both tired shoppers and those wanting a bite to eat. A local high school band might provide lunchtime entertainment.

Another form of entertainment at the Old Post Office is the clock tower. Ride the glass elevator up to the tower and, as reward, enjoy a 360 degree view of the city. It seems you can see forever from this vantage point. It is not as tall as the Washington Monument but it doesn't have the long waiting lines either. There are bells in the tower that are replicas of the bells of Westminster Abbey, a Bicentennial gift from England. They are rung only on special occasions. The tradition of celebrating New Year's Eve at the Pavilion has just begun. Thousands of people, like the people in Times Square on New Year's, come together on December 31 to say goodbye to old times and hello to the new.

Edward Durell Stone designed the Kennedy Center. This is a performing arts center that opened in 1971 and has been noted for performances in opera and by the symphony, as well as being the site for outstanding film and dance events.

The National Geographic Society was begun in the 1880's and now it has its own building on 17th and M Streets. Visitors love the dramatic displays in Explorer's Hall. There are many photographs in the building. One of the most outstanding photographic exhibits is of South American Indian tribes. There is another on rivers, and another on ships recovered from the ocean floor.

One of the most beautiful structures in the world is the Washington Cathedral. It stands on Mount Saint Albans and was erected to serve the country's need for state funerals and services. Different faiths use the building, which is intricately designed with stained glass and wood carvings, the result of thousands of hours of work by artisans. The bell tower is 300 feet high.

The National Shrine of the Immaculate Conception is the 7th largest church in the world. Services have been held here since 1927. It is built of Indiana limestone and can seat 3000 people. It is located near Catholic University.

Catholic University is but one notable university in this city. Others are Howard University, American University, Gallaudet College and Georgetown University.

Meridian Hill Park is another must for anyone wanting a spectacular view of the city. The park contains twelve acres of cherry trees and azaleas, as well as statues erected in honor of Joan of Arc, Dante and President Buchanen.

It was once thought that Georgetown would be the location of the new capital. Originally settled by immigrants from Scotland, Georgetown was called Dumbarton and later renamed for George Beall and George Gordon, owners of much of the property destined to be a prosperous seaport and tobacco trading city. However, despite the fact that the city flourished early and quickly, troubles came with the opening of the Chesapeake and Ohio Canal. The town's decline as a port cast a shadow over its promising future. Georgetown became part of the Federal District in 1871 and is now filled with houses made of brick and wood, galleries, and antique shops. Cobblestone streets contribute to its charm.

Near Georgetown University there's a plentiful supply of young people in search of food so there are fine restaurants and interesting gathering places, such as the American Cafe, a spot to eat with a market upstairs. Georgetown Park is a magnificent urban shopping center with a Victorian design. There is an atrium here. Shoppers wander over tile floors and rest on Victorian park benches with wrought iron arms and wooden-slat seats.

Just a half hour from Washington is Mount Vernon, President Washington's home. A visit to this well-kept country home gives one a good idea of the style of living during Washington's time. This is where he lived as a gentleman farmer, where he brought his bride, the wealthy Martha Dandridge Curtis, and where he is buried.

The estate did not come into public domain until 1858 when the Ladies Historical Association took it on. They have recreated George and Martha's era perfectly. The main house is surrounded by outbuildings and gardens. Inside the main house are the bedrooms, Washington's library, and music room with a harpsichord from London and a banquet hall.

The museum at Mount Vernon contains the soldierly belongings of the first president and many family belongings. Outbuildings, such as the shoe repair shop, were tended and slept in by slaves. They did all the work here, from shearing sheep to spinning wool to working the gardens.

George and Martha are buried here even though there was a great movement to have Washington buried in a tomb in the city of Washington, D.C. His family, however, disagreed and their wishes were honored.

Knowledge of the details of Jefferson's era is available for those who want to travel three hours to Monticello, his home in Virginia, or the University of Virginia, which he founded. He was the designer of both places and both give a sense of the time and the man. At Monticello, the gardens are being restored. Much that is inside the house was there when Jefferson was there so it is a typical rural colonial plantation, complete with stables and orchards.

Washington, D.C. has much to offer anyone interested in American history, architecture, art and today's politics. It is a city that was designed to be a capital and it has proven itself to be an outstanding city. Touring the historic buildings, visiting the monuments and memorials, or standing in the churches, parks and the backyards of people we've read about since we were children, it is impossible to avoid the knowledge that this is a place of importance. Things have happened here, and continue to happen, to impact the lives of millions of people. It is a city to know, honor and explore for everyone who wants to discover the origins and movement of this country.

Lincoln Memorial at Dusk